Original title:
Shade and Solace

Copyright © 2025 Creative Arts Management OÜ
All rights reserved.

Author: Elliot Harrison
ISBN HARDBACK: 978-1-80567-038-4
ISBN PAPERBACK: 978-1-80567-118-3

Sanctuary of the Silent Woods

In the woods where squirrels plot,
And each tree has secrets caught,
The owls hoot with laughter bright,
While raccoons plan their midnight flight.

Beneath a branch, a frog will croak,
Telling jokes that make me choke,
As fireflies dance in silly glee,
Lighting up the night for me.

A chipmunk juggles acorns near,
While rabbits giggle, full of cheer,
In this place, where all's a jest,
Nature's humor, truly blessed.

So here I sit, away from fuss,
With woodland friends, it's quite a plus,
In a realm where whimsy speaks,
And laughter flows for all the weeks.

The Caress of Faded Light

As the sun dips low, it winks at me,
Through branches swaying like a marquee,
The beams tickle leaves just like a tease,
Painting shadows that dance with ease.

A cat naps, thinking it's a king,
While crickets chirp, a nightly fling,
Fireflies flash, like stars on the ground,
In this soft glow, joy can be found.

Moths in their outfits, quite the show,
Flapping wings in a silly flow,
As if rehearsing for a grand play,
Under the fading light of day.

Wrapped in warmth of a light so sweet,
Nature's laugh is a rhythmic beat,
In this gentle dusk, I lose my cares,
Finding humor in the night's affairs.

Yearning for the Unseen

I wander paths where whispers hum,
In hopes of seeing what's to come,
But all I find are ninja bees,
Buzzing as they munch on leaves with ease.

The flowers giggle, they've cracked a code,
While ants march on their tiny road,
An animal parade, oh, what a sight!
Who needs a map when all feels right?

A cloud floats by, all dressed in fluff,
As if to say, "You've had enough!"
But I just grin, it's all a game,
In nature's chase, we're never the same.

So here I roam, with silly glee,
If only I could capture a tree,
Yet in this quest for what's not seen,
I find laughter in every green.

Nature's Softest Touch

In a green patch, where daisies bloom,
A butterfly flits, avoiding doom,
It stops to chuckle with a breeze,
Tickling petals, bringing to knees.

The wind plays tag with all the leaves,
Sowing giggles, where joy weaves,
A snail on a mission, slow yet game,
"Catch me if you can!" it seems to claim.

A flock of birds, they croon a tune,
Singing to the light of the moon,
Who knew nature had jokes in store,
With laughter echoing evermore?

So let the world around us spin,
In the cozy warmth, we'll dive right in,
With every rustle, every hush,
There's joy in nature's gentle rush.

Beneath the Bowing Boughs

Under branches that sway and bend,
Squirrels argue, their antics blend.
A bird drops a snack with a flap and a twirl,
While I dodge peanuts in a whirlwind swirl.

The tree whispers secrets, I giggle with glee,
A raccoon sneers, 'Oh, look at thee!'
With nature as witness, I dance like a fool,
Embracing the chaos, who knew it was cool?

Where Silence Blooms

In a garden where jokes take root,
Flowers chuckle in bright, silly suits.
The daisies exchange puns all day,
While the roses just blush, like, 'Okay, okay!'

A snail thinks he's speedy, oh what a hoot,
Waving at leaves, like 'I'm cute!' I'm cute!'
Nature's a stage, with laughter ablaze,
In this quiet spot, humor always stays.

The Sigh of Dusk

Dusk yawns wide, with comfy delight,
A cat sprawls out, claiming her right.
Crickets chirp jokes, the sun sets low,
In the backdrop, the fireflies glow.

A shadow passes, oh look, it's Fred!
Tripping over a toad, he tumbles ahead.
We all laugh as the evening unfolds,
With the world wrapped in giggles and gold.

Gentle Embraces of Night

As night giggles soft, starlight arrives,
Whispers of dreams where laughter thrives.
A stray moonbeam plays tag with a cloud,
While owls hoot riddles; they're rather loud!

Bats swoop by, with a playful shock,
'Did you hear the one about the old clock?'
Night tickles the senses, silly and bright,
In this cozy cocoon, everything feels right.

Illumination in the Quiet Places

In corners where dust bunnies play,
The light finds a way to sway.
A cat in a sunbeam, what a sight,
Chasing shadows, oh what a delight!

Old chairs creak with tales untold,
Where socks disappear, if I may be so bold.
Laughter echoes in whispered tunes,
As memories dance like animated balloons.

Comfort In the Unknown

A mystery lurks in the fridge's cold box,
Is it leftover pizza or advanced sock?
We stumble upon treasures, half-baked and keen,
Each bite a gamble, a culinary scene!

In closets unkempt, we find our past,
Old hats and toys, memories amassed.
With every surprise, our laughter erupts,
In the unknown, we find joy that disrupts.

The Radiance of Nightfall

As stars twinkle in the dark's embrace,
I trip on the curb, a comical chase.
Moonlit shadows play tag with me,
While I ponder life, sipping cold iced tea.

Crickets compose a symphony grand,
I wave at a bush, thinking it's my friend.
In twilight's humor, we all get along,
With fireflies leading the dance all night long.

Hiding In Gentle Glimmers

In the garden, a fairy-tale start,
But wait! A squirrel just stole my heart.
With shiny acorns and mischievous darts,
Nature's goofballs, these little parts!

Beneath the trees, secrets are stored,
Like where my missing sock has floored.
In glimmers of laughter, we find our cheer,
Turns out that fun was always near!

The Nest of Serenity

In a tree so tall, I found my snack,
A squirrel passed by, wearing a hat.
He waved his paws with quite the flair,
I chuckled loud, how can he care?

His nest was filled with acorn gold,
He offered me some, or so I'm told.
I took a bite, it tasted strange,
Guess I'll stick to chips; oh what a change!

The sun peeked down, a sassy grin,
The askew hat flew off in the wind.
I chased it down, quite the hot mess,
Our laughter echoed; can't help but guess!

So I lay down, my belly full,
While squirrels in hats play like a fool.
In this nest, who needs a plan?
With friends like these, we're in high demand!

Embracing the Partial Light

A half-lit room, where shadows dance,
I spilled my drink, oh what a chance!
The floor became a slip and slide,
As I took a leap with comical pride.

A cat just stared; eyes big and round,
I laughed so hard, I fell to the ground.
With every stumble, I found delight,
Embracing life in the quirky light.

Outside, the sun was playing peek,
With the clouds acting all so meek.
I thought of naps, but I just rolled,
Into the day, both warm and cold.

So here's to laughter, both loud and bright,
To sunshine's giggle and moonlight's bite.
When mishaps come, just give a shout,
For life's too funny to ever doubt!

The Enchantment of Solace's Nest

In a cozy nook, my comfy chair,
A frog in a top hat sat with flair.
He croaked a joke; I spilled my tea,
Oh, how he laughed, such glee to see!

Around us sprouted poppy bloom,
As bees all buzzed to clear the gloom.
They danced around, dressed in stripes,
One even tried to borrow my wipes!

With every sip and every laugh,
My worries shrank, a cozy half.
The frog stuck out a tiny tongue,
To catch a fly, a song unsung.

Together we feasted on crumbs of bread,
Each little joy, by a giggle led.
So if you find a frog in your best,
Join the laughter, and count your blessed!

Enclaves of Quietude

In a corner where shadows play,
The cat naps in a sunbeam sway.
The dog looks for a place to hide,
From a friend who's a very loud ride.

A squirrel plots his daring heist,
As a napkin floats like a feathery tryst.
Cushions pile in a cozy heap,
Laughing at secrets the corners keep.

Breathing Room Beneath the Sky

Under the tree, a picnic spread wide,
Ants march like soldiers, no one to guide.
While the ants have their marching parade,
I'm dreaming of snacks—who needs a charade?

The breeze whistles tunes, a funny old song,
While my sandwich performs a dance lasting long.
The blanket's gone rogue, it flips like a kite,
As laughter erupts, oh, what a delight!

The Comfort of Hidden Corners

In the nook where dust bunnies dwell,
A mystery forms like a whimsical spell.
A lost shoe begins to regale,
Tales of adventures on a wild trail.

The remote hides, playing peek-a-boo,
While I chase it in my bright polka-dot shoe.
A forgotten muffin sits soft and blue,
What a comrade in mischief, just me and you!

Timeless Stillness

In a chair that creaks with each gentle sway,
My thoughts bounce around—you can't hear them play.
An errant fly buzzes—what a delightful friend,
Like it's hosting a party that won't ever end!

The clock's ticking softly, but time doesn't care,
As I giggle at nothing while sinking into air.
The cozy vibe tickles, oh what a delight,
In this timeless escape, life feels just right.

Comfort in the Quiet Veil

Under the big ole tree, I sit,
Eating lunch, my favorite bit.
Squirrels dance, they steal my fries,
I laugh as they plot their little lies.

The sun's hot, it's blazing bright,
But I found a spot that feels just right.
The grass tickles, a soft embrace,
As I watch clouds drift, a lazy race.

A bird lands, starts to sing,
He thinks he's got the voice of a king.
But I can't help but find it odd,
Three catcalls from a lawn gnome god.

In this nook, the world feels fair,
Even with ants crawling up my chair.
I chuckle as I sip my drink,
Life's little joys help me to think.

The Shelter of Silent Leaves

Beneath the trees, I find my throne,
A leafy crown, I've overgrown.
The breeze whispers secrets, oh so sly,
While squirrels conspire, oh my, oh my!

A picnic basket, full of treats,
I plan to host a feast for sweets.
But here comes a raccoon, what a mess,
He steals my cookies with such finesse.

Nearby, a couple starts to argue,
About whose turn to bring the curfew.
I giggle quietly, sipping my tea,
In this nature drama, I'm the VIP.

So here I remain, in peace I dwell,
With leafy covers and stories to tell.
Nature's laughter fills the air,
Life's quirks are fun when you just don't care.

Embracing the Soft Umbra

In a hammock, swaying slow,
With a book that's got a dull flow.
The cat jumps up, purring loud,
His royal presence; I'm so proud.

The sun tries hard to beam and glow,
Yet here I dwell in shadows, oh so low.
A voice calls out, for no apparent reason,
I pretend it's a bug, in playful treason.

A picnic cloud floats by, so slow,
It's time for snacks, don't take too long though.
Here they come, my friends with glee,
Who knew they'd bring a cake for me?

We laugh and lie, both wide and free,
Sunny days are made for silly spree.
Together we bask in the gentle chill,
Creating memories that give me a thrill.

Echoes of Gentle Refuge

In a park where laughter bounces high,
I sit and watch the kites fly by.
A kid trips over, lands on his face,
Giggles follow him, oh what grace!

Butterflies flit, graceful yet bold,
While ants march on, a sight to behold.
A picnic spread with sandwiches stacked,
You'd think it's a tease—my fate is whacked!

The sunlight winks, throws patches around,
While I silently dodge some kid on the ground.
He's declared himself king of the spot,
But that's the best throne—I've got the shot!

So here I relax, with friends all around,
In this little haven, blissfully bound.
Life's little moments, so rich and sweet,
Make this sheltered nook, truly neat.

The Subtle Art of Being

In the park, the squirrels dance,
Chasing each other in a frantic prance.
A ladybug lands on my nose,
I sneeze, and off she goes!

Sunshine tickles my bare feet,
I grin at a pigeon, feeling the heat.
He puffs up, struts with pride,
While I'm flailing, trying to hide.

Clouds drift by, a fluffy parade,
As I contemplate the snacks I've made.
A sandwich thuds upon the ground,
I laugh, it seems the birds have found!

Trees wave hello in gentle breeze,
Their leaves laughing, aiming to tease.
I sip my drink, it spills, oh my!
The ants have staged a feast, oh why?

A Pause in the Chaos

In the kitchen, pots collide,
Pasta boils, noodles tried.
I check the sauce, oh what a mess,
My chef hat's not a great success!

The cat knocks down a cup of tea,
As I wade through my culinary spree.
A dash of salt, then some flour,
Oops! I created a doughy tower!

A phone call rings, it's my mother,
"Did you burn the toast?" oh brother!
I chuckle, "Not yet, give it time,"
This cooking gig is quite the climb!

Outside, the dog is on a roll,
Chasing his tail, oh what a goal!
I join him in this goofy dance,
Feeling life's quirks, taking a chance!

The Sweet Surrender of Silence

In a quiet nook, I find my place,
A dog snores loud, that's his grace.
The clock ticks slow, what a thrill,
I sip my tea, my heart stands still.

The fridge hums a gentle tune,
While I gaze out at the afternoon.
Birds squawk a raucous, silly show,
Life's absurdity starts to flow.

A spider spins a tale of thread,
Adds drama to my thoughts instead.
I laugh at my own twisted fate,
In silence, we all contemplate.

Outside, kids scream with delight,
While I stay cozy, tucked in tight.
Ah, the joy of watching chaos fly,
As I sip my tea and wave goodbye!

Saffron Skies and Emerald Depths

A sunset spills in hues of gold,
While I brave the grill, feeling bold.
Marshmallows flop and fall on cue,
S'mores are making their debut!

Fireflies wink, a sparkly crew,
As laughter erupts, what a view!
The dog chases shadows, he's quite the sight,
As I dodge the flames, oh what a night!

"Who knew cooking was this wild?"
I smile, feeling like a child.
The hammock swings, stars peek through,
I'm a master chef, who knew?

Under the surge of that saffron ray,
Life's quirks invite me to stay.
With laughter loud and joy that leapt,
I toast to moments I have kept!

The Solitude of Sun kissed Paths

On paths where sunlight dances bright,
A squirrel steals my sandwich with delight.
I chase him down, oh what a sight,
He laughs and scurries, a nimble flight.

The flowers smile, they know my plight,
They whisper tales of creams and bites.
I sit and ponder, not one to fight,
With crumbs aplenty, my meal feels right.

A ladybug joins this picnic spree,
She sips my juice, as bold as can be.
I let her stay, she's company free,
Together, plotting our fun jubilee.

But when the sun begins to fade,
I bid farewell, not one charade.
The critters laugh, this life's parade,
Until tomorrow, when games are played.

Whispers of the Earth

In a park where giggles rise and swell,
A duck waddles in, gives me a yell.
"Feed me fries, I'll cast a spell,"
But I bring seeds, and he starts to dwell.

The grass beneath my toes is green,
A worm crawls near with a sly routine.
"Join my dance," he asks, keen as can be,
We wiggle and tumble, a slippery scene.

The trees sway gently, cheeks aglow,
They gossip 'bout the folks below.
I nod along, though I don't quite know,
Why pinecones fall like falling snow.

As day turns dusk, the fun retreats,
The earth chuckles, sharing secret feats.
Tomorrow I'll return to my seats,
With fries for ducks and dancing beats.

Touch of Soft Breezes

A gentle breeze gives my hat a flip,
It sails away on a windy trip.
I chase it down, take a little skip,
While a nearby dog gives a comical grip.

The flowers wink, their colors bold,
Telling secrets that never get old.
"Wear polka dots!" they chirp, as I scold,
But fashion advice? Who needs to be gold?

A butterfly flits by with a grin,
It teases my hair; I give in.
We twirl together, a colorful spin,
In this wacky dance, we both win.

As the sun dips low, my hat's returned,
The breeze now laughs; my plans are churned.
With nature's chuckles, I feel so learned,
Who knew that joy is easily earned?

The Enfolding Nest

In a cozy nook, I take my seat,
A bird drops by for something sweet.
"Got any crumbs?" it tweets with glee,
I share my lunch; it's quite the treat.

The branches sway like they're in a dance,
The sun peeks in, giving it a chance.
"Stay for a story," I say, and prance,
Eager to share my goofy romance.

A squirrel joins with a nutsy flair,
He juggles acorns without a care.
The bird and I laugh at this wild affair,
And soon we're all lost in the air.

As evening falls, the stories flow,
With friends like these, the laughter will grow.
Under leafy canopies, we lay low,
In this world of whimsy, joy's the show.

The Embrace of Twilight's Caress

When the sun takes a bow with a wink,
The backyard squirrels start to drink.
Under a tree, they dance and prance,
While birds gossip, lost in a trance.

The garden chair creaks with delight,
As fireflies ignite the night.
A cat plots mischief, oh what a sight,
While frogs croak songs of pure fright.

The moon chuckles, a pale-faced moon,
As shadows play a silly tune.
In this circus of evening's fun,
Laughter lingers until day is done.

Each petal flutters, a dramatic flair,
While wind carries secrets through the air.
And all around, the world spins tight,
In this playful pause of light and night.

Nurtured by the Cool Sigh

A breezy whisper tickles my nose,
While garden gnomes deviously pose.
The flowers blush as they overhear,
The giggles of crickets drawing near.

Beneath the branches, ants start to march,
In perfect lines, a tiny arch.
They wave their flags of crumbly snack,
Winning the race, they never look back.

The owl hoots awkwardly, trying to rhyme,
As fireflies dance, they take their time.
A sneaky squirrel steals the last bite,
Oh, the drama of this cool night!

With shadows stretching their long, weird legs,
And raccoons plotting their sneaky dregs.
This lighthearted scene, a jolly surprise,
Weaves laughter through the starlit skies.

In the Arms of Whispering Winds

The leaves are gossiping, oh dear me,
They talk of squirrels and their wild decree.
While dandelions giggle, heads held high,
In a friendly tussle, oh my, oh my!

Wind carries tales, a funny old breeze,
Of roly-poly insects and cheeky freeze.
Beneath the arbor, shadows convene,
Where mushrooms sprout in a huddle routine.

A hat flies off, caught in a whirl,
As butterflies swoop in a twinkling swirl.
The jokes of nature bubble and brew,
In this quirky world where newcomers skew.

With every gust comes comedy grand,
Nature's script is drawn in a funny hand.
Laughter spills among branches and twigs,
In this lively play of winks and jigs.

Pathways to Still Waters

At the water's edge, a frog makes a splash,
Wishing the dragonflies would take a dash.
The fish giggle, hiding beneath the mire,
While reeds whisper secrets, climbing higher.

A turtle ambles, in no rush at all,
While cattails giggle, trying to sprawl.
The sun grins down with a warmish tease,
As clouds play hide-and-seek with the trees.

The ripples giggle with a bubbly sound,
As ducks perform plays in the round.
This stage of quiet, chaotic and neat,
Brings joy and laughter, oh, what a treat!

At every turn, a fun little mishap,
Nature's comedy, atop a warm lap.
Under the sky, where giggles collide,
In this tranquil place, all worries subside.

Softness in the Crevices

In the couch's deep folds, I do find,
Old snacks and lost toys, oh, what a bind!
A plush throne of comfort, yet crumbs reside,
Who knew that the sofa could be a wild ride?

Dust bunnies tumble like tumbleweeds,
Hiding secrets of laughter and funny deeds.
With remote control lost in the dark fold,
I uncover the stories that the cushions hold.

A cozy nook where giggles bloom,
The warmth of laughter fills every room.
I nestle in snug, with a soft blanket sweep,
And drift into dreams, chuckling deep.

In this hideaway, I reign supreme,
Master of comfort, the snack-loving dream.
So raise a toast to the couch's embrace,
Where every lump and bump has its place.

Calming the Restless Heart

A potted plant whispers with green sage,
Calming my heartbeat, like an old page.
It sways to a rhythm, oh so slow,
Almost as peaceful as a sitcom's flow.

I sip on chamomile, sweetened with glee,
Pretending I'm fancy, just sipping for free.
In a world where my worries take flight,
Tea stains on my shirt, but I feel alright.

The cat curls nearby, a round purring ball,
As I read all my texts from a bygone fall.
"Why can't you nap?" it silently stares,
While I wrestle with life and all of its flares.

But amid all the chaos, a chuckle will rise,
As I battle my heart with a feigned act of wise.
For laughter's the glue that binds us, you see,
In this calm little corner, it's just my cat and me.

Luminous Retreats

The lamp flickers on with a flashy twist,
Glowing like my hopes when I barely exist.
Each bulb's a star of a sitcom bright,
Gleaming with stories that laugh through the night.

My blanket fort stands, a fortress of cheer,
With fairy lights twinkling, the moment's so near.
A s'more-making mission, delicious and warm,
Even the marshmallows know how to charm.

Popcorn spills like the best sort of fight,
"Hey, give me some!" shouts the wild hungry bite.
This space of joy, where frowns turn to grins,
In fluffy clouds of cotton, we all remain kin.

With laughter resounding, I celebrate wit,
In this radiant haven, I quietly sit.
For every bright glimmer is a giggle unleashed,
And the best kind of fun is joy that won't cease.

Refuge Where Dreams Whisper

In my treehouse high where the squirrels dance,
I've created a world where dreams take a chance.
The leaves rustle softly, like giggles at play,
As I sip berry juice and watch clouds sway.

A sandwich of peanut butter, my esteemed choice,
Combining it all with a silly old voice.
"Gotta fuel up!" I declare with a grin,
As the vine swings behind, a wild, joyous spin.

The moon peeks in, throwing shade on my snack,
While I plot all the pranks I could plan for the crack.
With secret notes hidden in the soft bark,
I'll unleash all my jokes when it's finally dark.

So here's to the magic of childhood delight,
Where the dreams cling to laughter and the stars seem bright.
In this whimsical nook where silliness reigns,
I find my retreat from the world's pesky chains.

Cradled Under a Dome of Greens

In a leafy nook where squirrels play,
I found my lunch, or it found me today.
With every bite, a bird sang loud,
Who knew a salad could draw a crowd?

The sun peeked in with a cheeky grin,
While ants threw their very own picnic din.
I laughed aloud at the ruckus made,
Under this green, a fun charade!

Branches swayed like dancers bold,
As if to say, "Come join, behold!"
Yet pesky bees buzzed with their dance,
I swiftly backed off, no second chance!

So here I lay, in this leafy spa,
With nature's antics, I'm the star.
Cradled in greens, I munch away,
Life's whimsical feast, come, seize the day!

The Comfort of Lacy Shadows

Beneath the tree where shadows lace,
I found a seat, a perfect place.
A cat jumped by, with dread and charm,
Knocked over my drink, oh, what a harm!

Lacy patterns started to dance,
I giggled as they took their chance.
Whispers shared between the leaves,
And my tall iced tea, it quietly grieves.

The sun and clouds began their game,
Shadow puppets that never tame.
A butterfly sought my dinner plate,
Did it come to eat or just to relate?

With every shift, the light would play,
Turning my frown into a bouquet.
In this sweet spot, I feel like a queen,
In my refuge of whispers, vibrant and green!

Whispers of Dappled Light

In dappled spots where giggles hide,
A patch of sun, oh, what a ride!
I tripped on roots, did a little spin,
Nature won; it's got a grin!

The laughter echoed, bouncing around,
While twirling leaves danced on the ground.
Each flicker of light just loves to tease,
Reminds me, I'm not here to freeze!

A gentle breeze joined in the fun,
As squirrels debated who'd won the run.
Oh, the stories that chirps can weave,
In this little nook, there's nothing to grieve.

So I lay back, tracing the rays,
Counting the silly moments and days.
With whispers here that sparkle and tease,
Nature's laughter, a perfect breeze!

Veils of Comfort

Veils of green where the secrets grow,
A hammock swing, oh, what a flow!
In slow-motion, I drift away,
As boughs and breezes begin their play.

The sun pokes through with a golden nod,
While a toad croaks, looking quite odd.
He thinks he's a prince, perched cool on a log,
Yet I'm the one, in my comfort fog!

With laughter wrapped like a cozy quilt,
The tickling grass feels like a built.
Each giggle shared between trees and me,
Is the kind of joy that's pure jubilee!

So here I dwell, in this soft embrace,
Where every moment is a joyful chase.
Veils of giggles and breezy delight,
Wrap me up in the soft, silly light!

Tranquil Refuge Within

When the sun is blazing bright,
I seek my cozy nook,
A place where warm hugs sit tight,
In my beloved book.

Cats sprawl like fluff on the floor,
Chasing dreams of midnight snacks,
Each meow's a gentle roar,
As they plot their clever tracks.

The fridge hums a soothing tune,
My snacks dance in joyful array,
Here, I float like a balloon,
In my hideout, I will stay.

So when the world gets too loud,
And life's a circus act,
I'll just retreat, no need for a crowd,
In my tranquil, cozy pact.

Shadows That Heal

Beneath the trees, I find my play,
With squirrels doing ballet,
They frolic and leap without a care,
While I pretend not to stare.

A breeze whispers 'shhh' in my ear,
Like a secret shared with a dear,
Laughter echoes among the leaves,
As nature spins tales, it weaves.

Even the shadows wear a grin,
Dancing lightly on my skin,
In their company, I disappear,
A jester's heart brought near.

With every chuckle, I feel more light,
In this roam of whimsical fright,
For even shadows wear a jest,
Finding joy in this little quest.

The Light Within the Dusk

As day turns slow to twilight hue,
Fireflies join the dance anew,
They flicker like stars caught in flight,
Making the evening feel just right.

A bat swoops low, a comic bat,
With a nervous flap: 'What's up with that?'
While crickets chirp their silly tune,
Guess it's time for an evening swoon.

The moon peeks out, a cheeky grin,
As I pretend to be a kin,
To the owls hooting their wise old lore,
I chuckle under my breath—just one more!

So here I am, in dusk's embrace,
With laughter painting every space,
In these moments, my heart takes wing,
To the rhythms of night, my soul will sing.

A Veil of Stillness

At the edge of a field, butterflies glide,
Like tiny ships on a dreamy ride,
They linger a while, then zoom away,
Leaving giggles in the soft hay.

In the stillness, a toad softly sings,
With a voice that's fit for queens and kings,
It croaks of love, of summer's charms,
Creating peace with its croaking arms.

Beneath the hush, odd sounds arise,
Like a sneeze from a plump firefly's sighs,
Even the flowers nod off to sleep,
In this moment, tranquility runs deep.

So let the world rush and roar outside,
In this silent joy, I take my ride,
For in the calm, fun laughter we find,
The greatest treasures, unconfined.

When Dreams Take Shelter

In a cozy nook where thoughts reside,
Beneath a cheerful sunlight glide.
Pillows piled high, like clouds of fluff,
Naps are the treasure, sleep's just enough.

Snoring like a walrus, loud and proud,
Dreams drift away on a cotton cloud.
A grumpy cat meows, 'I'm not impressed!'
While visions of snacks put the mind to rest.

Frogs in pajamas leap with glee,
Twisting and turning, like a jubilee.
Caught in a dream where socks find pairs,
In a world where laughter fills the airs.

So let the day be filled with fun,
Until the setting of the golden sun.
In this fluffy realm, we all take flight,
For every dream is a comical sight.

Calmness in the Gloaming

Twilight slips on like a soft, warm coat,
As crickets play their cheerful note.
Fireflies dance, a flickering show,
While I ponder where lost socks go.

The sky's a palette of pink and gold,
Where tales of silly adventures unfold.
A chicken in shades struts like a star,
Clucking the secrets from near and far.

Laughter ripples through the evening air,
As rabbits perform in a light-hearted flair.
And if you listen, you might hear a tune,
From a roguish raccoon with a whimsical moon.

In this wayward hour, giggles resound,
As the world twirls, spinning round and round.
For calmness wraps us in a jolly embrace,
In the gloaming, all troubles erase.

In the Arms of the Elder Trees

Old trees chuckle with wisdom vast,
With branches that wave as saplings pass.
A squirrel debates whether to scold,
While shadows skip in the sunlight's gold.

With laughter echoes, they share their tales,
Of a mischievous raccoon who steals their gales.
A wise owl hoots, "Let's tell some jokes!"
As tiny ants march in military pokes.

Under a bough, the world feels bright,
While a porch swing sways in sheer delight.
Sipping lemonade, we toast the day,
To laughter and fun in the tree's play.

In their embrace, the worries flee,
Dancing with fruit flies in a breezy spree.
For adventures abound under leafy ceilings,
In the arms of the elder with funny feelings.

Beneath a Whispering Canopy

Beneath the leaves, secrets sway,
As evening whispers tales of play.
A squirrel in a top hat struts with flair,
Proposing tea parties in midair.

The shadows twirl in a giggling spree,
While with glee they collect the glee.
A hedgehog practices its stand-up act,
Joking of pricks with a charming pact.

Rippling laughter weaves through the trees,
As male cardinals flaunt their fine degrees.
A chorus of frogs joins in the chase,
Croaking the punchlines with perfect grace.

So here we sit, with joy amassed,
In a silly concert that's meant to last.
Underneath the jokes and leafy grasp,
Life's merry moments tightly clasp.

Twilight's Embrace

As day surrenders to night,
The fireflies dance, what a sight!
A squirrel steals my sandwich, oh dear,
Yet laughter lingers, it's quite clear.

The stars appear in a comical show,
They twinkle and wink, just like a flow.
I stumble on roots, oh such a fright,
But giggles erupt, it feels just right.

A blanket of laughter, around it I twine,
As shadows get silly, with mischief they shine.
A frog leaps and croaks, like it's telling a joke,
And I join in, laughing until I choke.

So here in the twilight, with giggles galore,
I find joy in chaos, forevermore.
With critters and chuckles, my heart feels so light,
In this whimsical dance of the fading daylight.

The Quiet Beneath the Canopy

Beneath the leaves, squirrels go wild,
Playing tag, just like a child.
A raccoon snickers with a shiny can,
And I can't help but laugh at his plan.

The branches creak with secrets untold,
A chipmunk's jokes, oh they're pure gold.
I sip my drink, but it spills on my shirt,
And everyone giggles; that's just dessert.

A breeze stirs the leaves, soft and light,
Whispers of chuckles fill the night.
Nature's humor, it's a delight,
As shadows giggle 'til dawn's first light.

In this leafy room, with shadows around,
Joy resides here, in laughter we're found.
So let's toast to the whims of the forest cheer,
With a wink and a chuckle, we welcome the year.

Serenity in the Shadows

In corners dark, where laughs are hid,
A cat naps on cushions, a furry kid.
The sunbeams peek and a voice sings out,
"Is that a mouse or just a funny shout?"

An owl hoots a comical tune,
While raccoons plot under the moon.
I step on a twig, it snaps with a crack,
And the critters all chuckle, that's just my luck!

The quiet whispers, but laughter does roam,
In the nooks and crannies, we find a new home.
A shadow might mutter, "You're quite the klutz,"
But it's all in good fun, no need for any fuss.

Underneath the giggles, peace finds its way,
In the soft, quiet dusk, we dance and we play.
With laughter as music, we glide through the night,
In this gentle embrace, everything feels right.

Echoes of Tranquility

In the depths of the woods, where silence sways,
Lies a chorus of critters, all singing their plays.
A deer tips its hat, with a grin on its face,
While the rabbits all chuckle, and join in the race.

The brook bubbles merrily, flipping a switch,
Where frogs leap in tune, each one is quite rich.
"Hop, hop!" they shout, it's a froggy parade,
I can't help but laugh at the plans that they've made.

Sunlight dabbles through, painting smiles so bright,
As the shadows shift gently, honoring night.
Worms wiggle with joy, underfoot they squirm,
And I laugh with a snicker, it's all just a term.

So here I bask in their joyful parade,
In nature's wild humor, my worries all fade.
Filled with chuckles and winks, I find, oh so deft,
In the echoes of giggles, I'm ever so blessed.

Beneath the Starlit Cover

The sky wears a blanket of twinkling light,
As we dodge the mosquitoes, oh what a sight!
With snacks in hand, we giggle and munch,
The stars above join in for the fun punch.

A raccoon peeks out, quite bold and brash,
Finding our popcorn, he makes a mad dash.
We shout in surprise, then all start to laugh,
A midnight snack thief? What a cheeky staff!

The moon grins down, a giant round face,
While we try to dance, but stumble in place.
Each twist and turn sends us laughing in glee,
Who knew starlit adventures could be so free?

Beneath this vast canvas, our spirits take flight,
In the company of stars, everything feels right.
With silly stories and a few gag jokes,
This night is a treasure, with shenanigans, folks!

Hush of the Evening Breeze

The evening whispers, a gentle caress,
We shiver in fancies, oh what a mess!
With fans and feathers, we wave at the flies,
Trying to look cool, but we can't tell no lies.

A chipmunk hops by, and we jump in surprise,
Does he think we're all nuts? Just look in our eyes!
He wiggles his tail, as if to decree,
That nature's got jokes, oh let it be free!

We sit on the porch, sipping drinks with a smile,
While ants plot a heist, oh what a sly file.
They march in a line, oh the chaos they bring,
"Is that a crumb?" they chant, as we laugh and sing.

As night drapes its cloak, we grin ear to ear,
These moments are treasures, so let's give a cheer.
For friendship and laughter, oh what a delight,
Let the evening breeze carry our joy through the night!

The Calm After the Storm

The skies have cleared, with a rainbow in sight,
We laugh as the puddles reflect pure delight.
Dancing in gumboots, what joy we can feel,
Splashes and giggles, the world is unreal!

A neighbor just slipped, oh what a great sight,
He's flailing his arms, a true comical flight.
With laughter erupting, we gather near by,
"Let's keep him dry!" someone shouts, oh my, oh my!

The clouds have retreated, they drift off with flair,
Leaving behind a canvas, freshened by air.
As we skip down the street, feeling quite bold,
Every raindrop's a story that needs to be told.

With warmth in our hearts and laughs that won't wane,
We gather our jokes, like a wild, joyful train.
In the calm after mayhem, we find what we seek,
A bond forged in chuckles, so vibrant, unique!

Lullabies of the Moonlit Grove

In the grove where the moon beams gently play,
We tiptoe through shadows, in twilight ballet.
A squirrel gives chase, we laugh as we flee,
He's got a sense of rhythm, oh can't you see?

The owls hoot softly, quite puzzled by us,
"Our nocturnal dance? What a thrilling fuss!"
With twirls and twinkles, we spin round and round,
In this nighttime festival, joys abound!

A twig snaps behind us, we turn with a scream,
But it's just a lost bunny, fulfilling a dream.
We giggle together, how silly we feel,
In this moonlit embrace, the world seems surreal!

So here in the grove, where laughter ignites,
We weave silly stories that dance through the nights.
With friends by our side, and the stars up above,
We cradle our moments in friendship and love!

Beneath the Boughs of Serenity

In a garden thick with leaves,
A squirrel forgot his keys.
He searched beneath the boughs,
While ants called him a clown.

A bird joined in his quest,
Chirping loudly, doing its best.
"Don't worry, friend, keep your chin!"
"Just remember where you've been!"

Laughter echoed in the trees,
With honeybees buzzing with ease.
Together they formed a band,
Forgetting the keys they planned.

At dusk, with glowing light,
They danced and laughed, what a sight!
And when the moon began to rise,
Even the owl had to sigh.

The Calm Between the Sunbeams

Between the sunbeams, they play,
A cat dodges rays during the day.
With every leap, a twist and a turn,
Chasing her tail—oh, when will she learn?

A lizard on a rock watches her dance,
Thinking, "Is this cat trying to prance?"
While the tortoise moves slow and steady,
Saying, "I'll race, but I'm really not ready!"

The flowers giggle, oh so bright,
As shadows form in the fading light.
The breeze teases, a tickle of air,
While butterflies laugh without a care.

At the end of the day, when the light does fade,
The critters all gather—no plans were made!
In the calm of the twilight, they find their jest,
A humorous world in a cozy nest.

Tranquil Shadows on Woven Paths

On woven paths, the shadows creep,
Where turtles and rabbits make their leap.
"Hello!" says one with a goofy grin,
"Why walk fast when we can just spin?"

A hedgehog with shades relaxes the most,
While squirrels plot their nutty toast.
They chuckle at clouds puffing by,
And wish they could float up to the sky.

In golden hours, there's laughter shared,
As crickets perform, totally unprepared.
The shadows dance with a twirl and sway,
Finding humor in the end of the day.

When night arrives, they don their hats,
Sharing tales of their backyard chats.
With giggles and glee, they call it a night,
In tranquil dreams, all feels just right.

A Solitary Retreat in Green

In a patch of green, with a wink of blue,
A frog strums a tune, feeling brand new.
With no one around for a very long while,
He croaks out a rhythm, and thinks he's got style!

A bumblebee buzzes with beats so fine,
Wondering why frogs can't share a line.
He's tried it before, but no one can see,
The brilliance of mixing, oh, why can't it be?

The willow tree sways, and chuckles aloof,
As a snail, in slow motion, just heads for the roof.
"This is my retreat; all is good here,
I'll take my time—there's nothing to fear!"

With laughter and joy, they come to agree,
Nothing's more fun than being so free.
In their secret nook, everything's neat,
In this happy retreat, they feel life's sweet.

Nestled Between the Moments

In the nook of a cozy chair,
I ponder the dust in my hair.
A cat on my lap, purring sweet,
The world's a buffet, and I'm just a treat.

The cookies are calling, I'm losing my fight,
The dishes can wait—who needs that delight?
With chocolate in hand, I declare, it's divine,
I've mastered the art of relaxing just fine.

The clock strikes again, how could it be so?
Time bends like a noodle, fast but so slow.
With naps as my hobbies and snacks as my art,
Being lazy's a craft, it's a skill not a part.

So here's to the couch, to my blanket so grand,
May this moment forever ooze under my hand.
Each laugh tugs the heart, what a splendid parade,
In my fortress of comfort, oh how I have stayed!

Under a Muffled Sky

Beneath a cloud that looks like a sheep,
I chase down my dreams, but they're hard to keep.
With sandwiches dancing in my picnic basket,
I lose to the ants—man, they're such a rascal!

Each twinkling star plays hide and seek,
While I trip over roots, feel a bit meek.
A squirrel strolls by with a nut in his hand,
And I swear he's judging my picnic's poor brand.

A soda can fizzles; it sounds like a laugh,
As I watch my sandwiches make a quick half.
A bee buzzes by, it gives me a wink,
I plead with my shins not to blink or to stink.

Muffled giggles drift up from the grass,
As the day whispers jokes that are sure to last.
Under this canopy, I feel quite the spy,
My heart full of joy, with a grin, oh so sly!

The Essence of Twilight's Grip

Twilight's a painter, with brushes of gold,
She colors my worries, now nothing feels bold.
With neighbor's loud music creating a rift,
I'm just here for snacks—my favorite gift!

Fireflies flicker, they've got moves of a pro,
I'd join their dance, but my feet say no-go.
An ice cream cone drips, I'm wearing it proud,
In this nighttime gala, I stand out in the crowd.

The moon winks at me, is he up for a joke?
I laugh at the clouds, and I swear they all spoke.
With shadows that giggle under the swings,
The world takes a bow, and my heart brightly sings.

In the quiet of dusk, there's a chuckle so deep,
It creeps into dreams like a smile in sleep.
So here's to the night and the chuckles it brings,
In the embrace of twilight, each joy gently swings!

Solitude's Gentle Whisper

In the corner of silence, I find a tall chair,
Where whispers of mischief waltz through the air.
A sock on the floor seems to plot with a shoe,
While I sip my tea, feeling rather askew.

The clock has a tick that mocks me just right,
It knows I could never leave bed in the night.
With crumpets performing their wobbly dance,
I chuckle aloud, as they leap in a trance.

Outside, the wind seems to ruffle my hair,
As I play with my thoughts, like a kid beyond care.
The pantry, a treasure, I dive in with glee,
It's all about snacks when no one's here but me!

But loneliness warms like a sunbeam's soft glow,
Each giggle and chuckle gives way to the flow.
With whispers and crumbs, I'm the queen of my space,
In this gentle retreat where I can truly embrace!

A Haven of Fleeting Moments

In a corner of my yard, a gnome does stand,
With a grin and a shovel, he claims the land.
He whispers secrets, but only to bees,
Who gossip in buzzes about their wild fees.

The flamingo floats, a plastic delight,
Practicing yoga from morning to night.
It's quite a sight, though one might ask how,
That bird holds a pose and doesn't bow.

A cat sprawled out, soaking up rays,
Dreams of conquering her lazy maze.
With a twitch of the ear, she plots her attack,
On a fly that dares to dive and then back.

While squirrels play poker on the old oak's bark,
In a game of chance, it's a real lark.
With acorn chips and a wager of seeds,
Laughing out loud at their neighbor's misdeeds.

Respite in the Half-Light

Beneath the porch light, moths flit and sway,
Dancing with purpose but lost on the way.
To candles and lanterns that tease them with glow,
A boisterous ball that nobody knows.

The fireflies twinkle like they're in a race,
Drawing paths across the night's secret space.
A race to the fridge for the last piece of pie,
Murmurs of victory, what a sly guy!

Old chairs creak tales of forgotten delight,
Of socks lost in laundry by morning light.
They chuckle and groan at the stories they've seen,
Of naps taken too long and great spoons of cream.

In shadows that dance, all the funny falls,
Like a tumble of laughter that wobbles and sprawls.
As the moon whispers jokes to the stars up above,
Nature's comedy night, who needs more love?

Caressed by the Hush of Nature

A frog croaks a tune by the pond's edge bright,
Complaining of bugs that vanish from sight.
He hops on a lily, with gusto and grace,
A splash and a belly flop—what a wild chase!

The trees have their gossip, all rustle and sway,
Chatting of breezes and the critters' play.
With a whoosh and a giggle, they tickle the air,
Creating a chorus of chuckles everywhere.

The old tortoise marches, so slow and so proud,
Keeps his own time, not afraid of the crowd.
While the sprightly hare zooms by in a flash,
Says, "Every second counts, let's have a big bash!"

In the space where the wild stories flow and glide,
Each rustle and chirp works up a great ride.
The dusk is a stage, and we're all in the scene,
Laughing at life, yeah, it's all so serene!

Lush Hiding Places of the Mind

In a garden of dreams, where thoughts like weeds grow,
High on a thought cloud, pausing to show.
A patch of wild daisies pop up with a grin,
They plot a wild journey, alas, where to begin?

The old rocking chair creaks a tune so grand,
As if to remind me of a faraway land.
With a drink in my hand and a laugh on my tongue,
I'm off to the races where the silliness sprung.

The walls tell stories, of laughter and play,
Echoes of giggles that never decay.
A cupboard of secrets, snacks, and lost socks,
With memories stored like unexpected rocks.

Each corner a sanctuary, a hideaway joke,
With puns in the shadows, like whispers bespoke.
The journey is merry, let's take an odd turn,
For each twist and each bend, there's more fun to learn!

Tucked Away in Nature's Arms

In a grove where the squirrels play,
I found my heart, bright as the day.
Chasing giggles, just like a breeze,
Hiding from chores, oh, such sweet tease.

Beneath a tree, I spied a hare,
He twirled in circles, without a care.
I dared to join, and what a sight,
Two fools dancing, oh, pure delight.

A branch overhead, gave us a seat,
While ants paraded, with dainty feet.
Together we laughed, 'neath leaves so lush,
Our worries departed, in joyful hush.

So come, dear friend, let's take a break,
From life's fierce race, for nature's sake.
We'll bask in joy, with laughter's ring,
In this garden of bliss, where love takes wing.

A Pact with Peace

Over tea with a butterfly's wing,
I made a promise, quite daring thing.
With giggles of flowers swaying bright,
I traded noise for lime-green light.

In talks with bees, buzzing like pros,
We laughed at how the garden grows.
I swore off blunders, at least for an hour,
While snacking on daisies, I felt the power.

A pact declared, with all things sweet,
To wear a smile, and dance on my feet.
With crickets composing, a tune just right,
My heart did a jig, under stars so bright.

So here's to the moments, funny and rare,
Where peace finds a way, without a care.
Let laughter ring true, with the moon's soft tease,
For joy multiplies, like a critically acclaimed cheese.

Oasis of the Soul

In a puddle of sunshine, I took my seat,
With frogs croaking jokes, so offbeat.
They ribbited puns while I munched on grass,
Creating a haven, for time to pass.

With lizards debating who's faster at sun,
And squirrels stealing moments, oh what fun!
I joined their circus, a one-man show,
Complete with a tumble, falling down low.

In shimmering air, with no worries in tow,
The world felt lighter, like driftwood in flow.
With every chuckle, I found a new bliss,
In this quirky escape, I sealed with a kiss.

So let's trade the grind for a whimsical stroll,
Through forests of laughter, come join the roll.
An oasis awaits, just behind the trees,
In the playful whispers of the buzzing bees.

Dances beneath Drifting Clouds

I spun with the clouds, who pirouetted above,
Crafting a stage made of daydream and love.
With twirls of cotton, I played in their grace,
Like a kid in a circus, lost in the space.

The wind blew a tune, I couldn't ignore,
As it tickled my ears, I begged for more.
Together we laughed, with each jolly gust,
While leaves whispered secrets, in breezy trust.

Down to the ground, I collided with glee,
Doing the worm with a chubby bumblebee.
Our steps were delightfully out of sync,
In this dance of oddities, we giggled and winked.

As sunlight draped, we bantered along,
With clouds in a row, we felt so strong.
In this frolicsome moment, let merriment flow,
For in laughter, we thrive, like saplings in glow.

Whispers of Dappled Light

Under the leaves, a squirrel does prance,
Chasing his tail in a comical dance.
Sunlight flickers, a game of tag,
While ants conspire and the insects brag.

In the cool of the green, a picnic's alive,
With sandwiches flying as bees all arrive.
Lemonade spills, a laugh erupts loud,
As the blanket shifts under a wiggly crowd.

A shadowy figure, the neighbor's old cat,
Lays sprawled out wide—was that once a mat?
The sun's golden rays begrudgingly tease,
As the cat pretends not to care, just to please.

In this lively spot, we share our wit,
With jokes that tumble, a humorous fit.
With light-hearted jabs, and laughter galore,
We bask in this dance, forever to soar.

Beneath the Canopy's Embrace

Beneath the vast gloom where jokes can hide,
A raccoon steals snacks with unapologetic pride.
While thrushes chirp sweet melodies clear,
A frog joins in, his croak bringing cheer.

Under the branches, the shadows do play,
Bouncing and bending in a whimsical way.
Laughter erupts as we dodge a rain drop,
While squirrels giggle and say, "Never stop!"

With ants in a line and a cloud of sweet flies,
The grass tickles toes as we tell little lies.
"Was that a tree born to dance?" we ponder,
While the sun peeks through our hearts, we wander.

As laughter fades out, rustling leaves stay bright,
It's the silly moments that bring us delight.
With candy wrappers fluttering here and there,
We'll forever treasure this joyous affair.

Secrets in the Twilight Cove

In the hush of the night, when the giggles soar,
Fireflies twinkle, oh what's in store?
Behind the great trees, shadowy figures conspire,
Wishing for mischief, we fuel their desire.

The crickets join in, percussion so fine,
As whispers of antics do brightly entwine.
"Did you see that?" a shout from our friend,
Who swears he saw what he cannot defend.

The pond reflects mischief, moonbeams aglow,
We ponder the truth of the tales that we know.
With laughter so pure and smiles so wide,
We whisper our secrets, the night, our guide.

As stars poke their heads out, sharing their fate,
We skip through the twilight, and it's never too late.
In the soft of the dark, we're silly and bold,
While secrets abide in the stories retold.

Hushed Corners of the Heart

In corners of calm where grass seems to sway,
A young child gabs, a whirlwind of play.
"Look at my shadow!" he chuckles with glee,
As it leaps and bounds, oh wait, is it me?

With ice cream in hand, a drippy delight,
It lands on his nose, oh what a sight!
Giggles erupt in this tranquil retreat,
As friends gather 'round, we're never discreet.

The secrets we share, both silly and grand,
Have roots in the joy that we cherish and band.
With tickles and tales, the laughter flows free,
In tender retreats, love's warm jubilee.

As shadows grow long and the day dims away,
We promise to mingle and meet come what may.
In hushed, cozy corners, our hearts gently weave,
A tapestry bright, in humor, we believe.

Twilight's Gentle Embrace

When evening whispers soft and low,
The world begins its sleepy show.
With fireflies dancing, up they flit,
While crickets play their nightly skit.

The cat snickers, stalking shadows near,
While dogs prepare to chase their fear.
In twilight's grip, all worries cease,
As laughter bubbles, life's a breeze.

A squirrel sneaks, avoiding glance,
With acorns hidden in a dance.
We giggle at the clumsy flops,
And watch the antics, even hops!

So, grab your snacks, let troubles fade,
In evening's glow, let joy invade.
A silly world, where chuckles reign,
In twilight's arms, we dodge the mundane.

The Coolness of Retreating Sun

As day bids farewell with a wink,
The sun slips low, and we all think.
Did I leave my socks on the line?
Oh wait, it's dinner time—divine!

With shadows stretching, we play tag,
While ants march on, a tiny brag.
The lemonade sits, ice cubes clink,
And old man Fred spills while we blink!

The sun rolls down, a fiery ball,
We wave goodbye, then heed the call.
Ice cream cones in hand, we cheer,
For every sunset brings good cheer!

So come my friends, let's take a chance,
And laugh while twilight starts to dance.
Under this glowing, fiery crown,
We'll share our tales as the sun goes down.

Stillness Behind Silvered Branches

Amidst the leaves, a secret hid,
Where giggles laugh and worries slid.
Behind the trunk, we spy and peek,
As squirrels plan a nutty sneak!

Branches sway, a gentle tease,
While birds conspire with the breeze.
A game of hide-and-seek unfolds,
With tales of laughter, mischief bold.

We sit awhile, on mossy ground,
Sharing secrets in whispers sound.
Old tree trunks shrug, what tales they know,
As laughter echoes, soft and low.

So leap between the roots and wild,
With nature's joy, forever mild.
In shaded corners, we take our chance,
To spin our tales in carefree dance.

Murmurs from a Shaded Overlook

High on the hill, we take our place,
To watch the world at a steady pace.
Beneath the trees, we take a seat,
And snack on cookies, oh what a treat!

The breeze tells stories, sweetly laid,
Of gnomes and fairies in sun and shade.
While flowers gossip, petals sway,
And butterflies giggle, flit away.

A squirrel performs, a stand-up set,
While we all chuckle, can't forget.
With sun above and joy all around,
In simple moments, bliss is found.

So bring your pals and snacks galore,
Here in the shade, we can't ignore—
Life's little joys and silly pranks,
In nature's theater, we give our thanks.

www.ingramcontent.com/pod-product-compliance
Lightning Source LLC
Chambersburg PA
CBHW072141200426
43209CB00051B/253